ANIMAL ABILITIES

RATS

Anna Claybourne

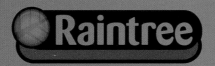

Chicago, Illinois

© 2013 Raintree
an imprint of Capstone Global Library, LLC
Chicago, Illinois

To contact Capstone Global Library, please call 800-747-4992, or visit our web site www.capstonepub.com

Edited by Laura Knowles, Abby Colich, and Diyan Leake
Designed by Victoria Allen
Original illustrations © Capstone Global Library Ltd 2013
Illustrated by HL Studios
Picture research by Elizabeth Alexander
Originated by Capstone Global Library Ltd
Printed and bound in China by CTPS

17 16 15 14 13
10 9 8 7 6 5 4 3 2 1

Library of Congress Cataloging-in-Publication Data
Claybourne, Anna.
   Rats. -- (Animal abilities)
Cataloging-in-Publication data is available at the Library of Congress.

ISBN (PB): 978 1 4109 5248 6
ISBN (HB): 978 1 4109 5241 7

Acknowledgments
We would like to thank the following for permission to reproduce photographs: Alamy pp. 7 (© Visual&Written SL), 12 (© Juniors Bildarchiv GmbH), 19 (© Mary Evans Picture Library); Corbis pp. 20 (© Bettmann), 21 (© Elke Van De Velde), 22 (© Wolfgang Flamisch), 25 (© Emmanuel Kwitema/Reuters), 29 left (© Michael Durham/Minden Pictures); FLPA p. 18 (© Erica Olsen); Getty Images pp. 24 (Yasuyoshi Chiba/AFP), 26 (Pierre Verdy/AFP); Nature Picture Library pp. 4 (© Warwick Sloss), 6 (© Gary K. Smith), 13 (© Steimer/ARCO); Newscom p. 16 (Splash News); Photoshot pp. 5 (NHPA/Daniel Heuclin), 10 (BSIP); public domain/Joseph Smit p. 28; Science Photo Library pp. 11 (Patrick Landmann), 27 (George Steinmetz); Shutterstock pp. 8 (© Volkova), 9 (© Artmim), 14 (© constructer), 15 (© Oshchepkov Dmitry), 29 right (© Elena Larina). Design feature of a rat silhoutte reproduced with permission of Shutterstock (© Potapov Alexander).

Cover photograph of a rat reproduced with permission of Shutterstock (© Pakhnyushch).

Contents

Some words are shown in bold, **like this**. You can find out what they mean by looking in the glossary.

Meet the Rat

Rats are everywhere! These small, furry **rodents** live almost anywhere humans live as well as in the wild. Rats are tough and intelligent, and they can survive on almost any food. This is how they have managed to spread all over the world.

Common rats

When you think of a rat, it is probably a brown rat or black rat. These are the two most common **species** (types) in towns and cities. Black rats are usually smaller and darker than brown rats and have longer tails. A brown rat can be 20 inches (50 centimeters) long from nose to tail—the length of a small dog!

A brown rat sniffs around a garbage can at night.

The giant bushy-tailed cloud rat is from the Philippines in Asia.

The rat family

There are many other kinds of rat, such as the rare and strangely named nonsense rat from India! The African giant pouched rat is one of the biggest of all, reaching nearly 40 inches (1 meter) long, including its tail.

RAT NICKNAMES

Rats have a lot of nicknames:
Brown rat: *Common rat, street rat, sewer rat, Norway rat*
Black rat: *Roof rat, ship rat, house rat*

Being a Rat

Most rats are **nocturnal** and come out at night to look for food. During the day, they hide away in their dens, burrows, or nests.

Brown rats are good at swimming and often live in sewers.

Where is home?

In the countryside, rats may make burrows or nest in trees. In cities and towns, they live in lots of places, such as under sheds, in attics, or in barns. They can also live in gardens, subway stations, and garbage dumps.

Lots of rats!

Rats are social animals that live in groups. If they have enough food, there can be hundreds of rats living together. Each rat only lives for around 1 to 2 years, but rats have a *lot* of babies, so their numbers can grow fast. A female rat gives birth up to 10 times a year, with around eight babies (called pups or kittens) in each litter.

ARE RATS ENDANGERED?

A few types of rats are **endangered**, such as the nonsense rat, which only lives on a few islands in India. But black and brown rats are so common that in some places they can threaten other species.

This is a mother brown rat with a litter of pups.

Rat Bodies

Rats are **mammals**. They are warm-blooded, covered in hair, and feed their babies on milk.

In this picture of a brown rat, you can see the main parts of a typical rat's body.

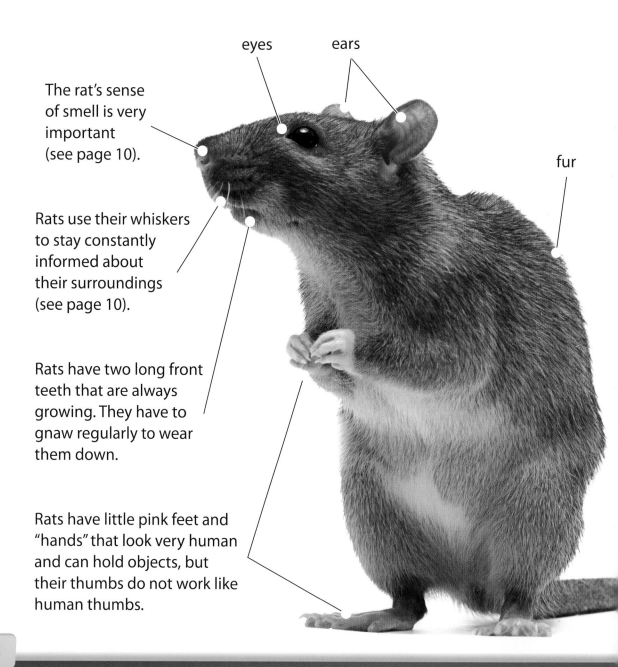

eyes

ears

fur

The rat's sense of smell is very important (see page 10).

Rats use their whiskers to stay constantly informed about their surroundings (see page 10).

Rats have two long front teeth that are always growing. They have to gnaw regularly to wear them down.

Rats have little pink feet and "hands" that look very human and can hold objects, but their thumbs do not work like human thumbs.

A TIGHT SQUEEZE

A medium-sized rat can wriggle through a gap that is about the width of a quarter. This is why it can be hard to keep rats out of houses — they can squeeze under doors, between floorboards, or through other small gaps.

A rat's tail has no fur on it. It is used for controlling body temperature and balance. A few types of rat can also use their tails to hold onto things.

Rats often use their hands to hold onto food as they eat it.

Rat Brains and Senses

Rats are not the smartest of all animals, but they do well on intelligence tests set for them by scientists. They have some pretty amazing sensing abilities, too.

Sensing the world

Rats cannot see very well, but they have an amazing sense of smell, which they use to find food, sniff out danger, and recognize other rats. They also have very sharp hearing. They can detect quieter and higher sounds than humans can, so they can hear each other's high-pitched squeaks.

A rat's whiskers are super-sensitive. They can detect different textures and surfaces and even pick up sound waves from the air. Rats often run around in dark, narrow spaces such as burrows, so they use their whiskers to feel everything around them as they go.

A rat's whiskers brush against everything it runs past and send signals to its brain.

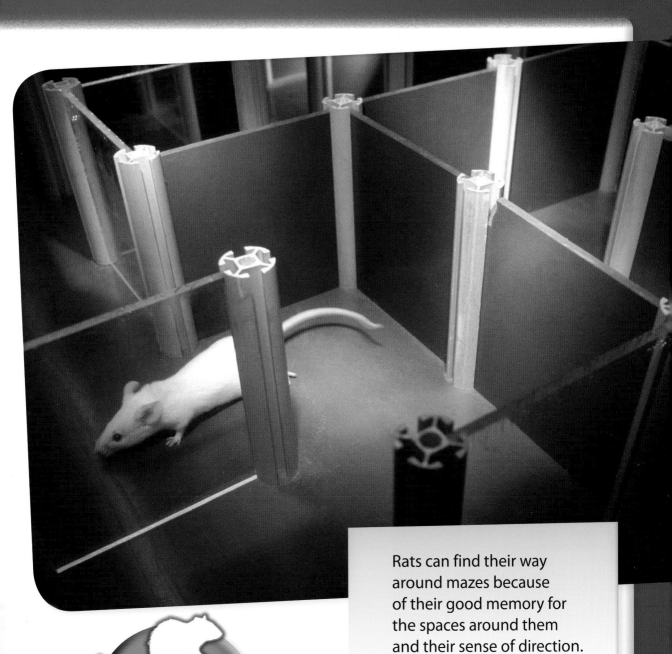

Rats can find their way around mazes because of their good memory for the spaces around them and their sense of direction.

HOW DO WE KNOW?

One rat intelligence test found that if rats think they cannot solve a puzzle with a big reward, they will choose not to take the test and opt for a small reward instead. This means rats have a skill that is unusual for animals—they can think about their own knowledge and abilities, the way humans can.

Rat Packs

Rats usually live in small groups, called **packs** or clans. A pack can be all male, all female, or a mixture. Rats rely on their pack, and being close to other rats is very important to them. They often snuggle up together and **groom** and wash each other.

A pack of rats cuddle up together to sleep.

Who's in the pack?

Female packs contain a handful of mothers and their babies. They share a nest and help each other care for their pups. Meanwhile, male rats roam around in their own groups or sometimes join with females to make a mixed pack.

No, I'm the boss!

Every rat has its own role in the pack. Rats chase, nip, groom, and play-fight to remind each other of everyone's position. For example, a **dominant** rat can pin another rat down and stand over it, to show he is in charge.

Pet rats will play the way that rats do in the wild.

HOW DO WE KNOW?

It is hard to study rats in dark burrows, sewers, or basements, so scientists learn about rat packs by watching **captive** or pet rats. However, their behavior is probably slightly different. For example, scientists think wild rats fight less because they can easily escape from each other.

Rat Chat

Rats "talk" to each other all the time. They do this in two main ways: smell and sound.

Sniff... sniff...

Rats can easily tell their pack members from other rats by their smell. Also, each rat leaves a trail of urine (pee) wherever it goes. It contains smelly chemicals called **pheromones** that tell other rats whether it is male or female, its age, and even its role in its pack. Rats have a special second nose for detecting pheromones. It is called the vomeronasal organ, or VNO, and is found in a tiny passageway just inside the rat's main nose.

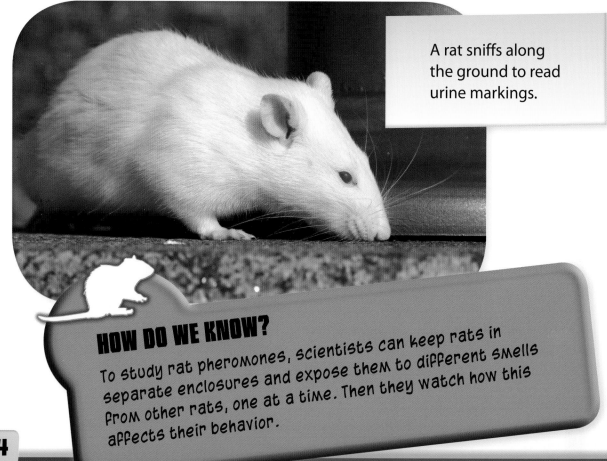

A rat sniffs along the ground to read urine markings.

HOW DO WE KNOW?

To study rat pheromones, scientists can keep rats in separate enclosures and expose them to different smells from other rats, one at a time. Then they watch how this affects their behavior.

Squeeeeak!

Just like in cartoons, rats really do squeak. In fact, they make all kinds of sounds, including chattering, chirping, and hissing. Many are **ultrasonic**—too high pitched for humans to hear. Some scientists say rats even seem to laugh when they are tickled!

SPEAK RAT

Sound	Meaning
Loud teeth chattering	I'm feeling anxious.
Loud shriek	Ouch!
Long squeak	I don't like this, stop it!
"Bruxing," or gently grinding teeth	Ahh, I'm relaxed and content.
Hissing	Don't mess with me!
Short squeak	I'm play-fighting!
Bwip!	I'm being groomed by another rat!

Rats sniff and squeak to get information about the world around them.

Learning

All animals have some abilities they do not have to learn, such as swallowing food or blinking. These abilities are called instincts. But some animals, such as rats, are also very good at learning new things.

Pet rats can learn to do tricks.

Growing up

Baby rats learn their own mother's smell, so they can tell her apart from other rats. They also learn which foods are safe to eat as well as the pattern of pathways around their nest.

HOW DO WE KNOW?

Scientists began making mazes for rats around the year 1900. One early experimenter, Willard Small, built a model of the human-sized maze at Hampton Court Palace in London. He found that rats could solve the maze easily and quickly became better and better at doing so.

In lab tests, rats can find their way through a maze, learn the route, and remember it. They may have developed this skill because they have to remember where all their pathways or burrows are in the wild.

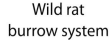

Wild rat burrow system

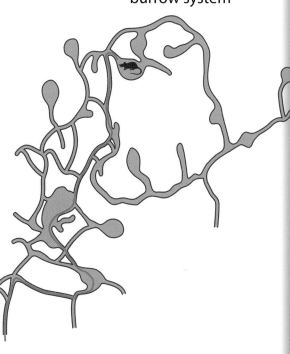

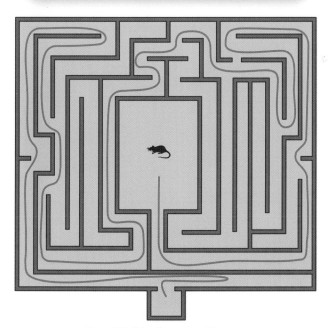

Small's Hampton Court rat maze

Adapting

Adapting means changing to suit the situation you are in. Rats are amazing at this, especially brown rats. They can easily switch between different homes, foods, and climates. This is one reason why rats are so good at surviving.

Ratty roommates

Rats have existed for much longer than humans. But when humans first appeared and began building homes, growing crops, and using fires to cook and keep warm, it gave rats a free ride. Many rats adapted to living with humans and found they could use our warm homes, food supplies, and tasty leftovers.

This brown rat is helping itself to some leftovers.

Rats on a journey

As humans spread around the world, rats went with them, hitching a ride on boats and grain wagons. Rats coped easily with the new foods and surroundings. Many other animals, such as pandas, cannot do this because they are suited to only one particular place or lifestyle.

This old illustration shows rats making their way to shore along a ship's ropes.

RAT FOOD

Rats will eat almost any food, including:
- fruits and vegetables
- plants
- meat
- nuts and seeds
- chocolate
- frogs
- small mammals
- insects
- bones
- any human garbage or leftovers
- carrion (dead animals)
- vomit...
- ...and even animal poo!

Pests or Pets?

As far as humans are concerned, rats are both pests and pets! When they live alongside us, rats can make a terrible mess. They chew wood, paper, and electrical wires to make their nests and to keep their teeth short. And they go to the bathroom everywhere!

This is a scene from the days of the Black Death, when carts collected dead bodies in the streets.

Deadly diseases

One reason why you should not touch wild rats is that they can carry dangerous diseases. The worst example ever was the bubonic plague, or Black Death. Rats caught the disease, then fleas spread the plague germs from rats to humans in their bites. In the 1300s, the plague spread across Europe, killing 25 million people.

HOW DO WE KNOW?

Scientists did not discover what caused the plague or how it spread until the 1890s, when new microscopes allowed them to learn much more about germs and how they work.

Pet rats

Rats can be great pets because they are smart and social. Like dogs, they get very attached to their owners. Pet rats were first bred from brown rats, but they now come in many varieties and colors. Some are even bald!

Pet rats usually live in cages, but some owners carry them around with them.

Lab Rats

Rats have been used in lab experiments for almost 200 years to study germs and diseases, intelligence, and much more. Since they are similar to us in some ways, they are also used to test medicines.

Meet the lab rat

Lab rats were bred from brown rats, but they now look very different. They are mainly white, and there are several different types, or **strains**:

- Wistar rat: A lab rat that is an albino (has little or no natural color) and is for general use

- Sprague Dawley rat: A white, calm, easygoing rat

- Zucker rat: A very hungry, fat rat used to study **obesity**.

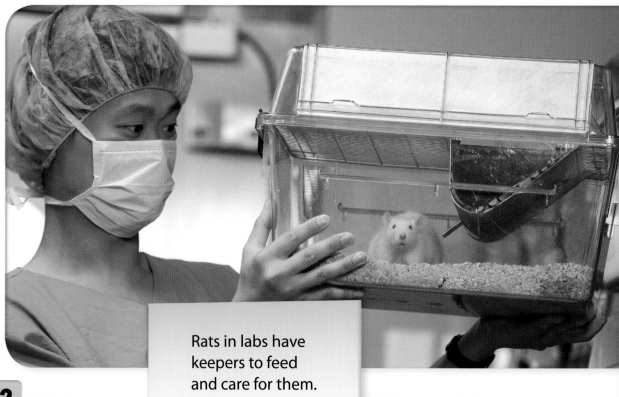

Rats in labs have keepers to feed and care for them.

IS IT CRUEL?

Some people say using any animal in science labs is cruel and wrong. Others say it is OK if the rats are treated well. Some rat experiments, such as medical tests, save human lives. Lab rats are specially bred and would not have a life at all otherwise — though it is not a natural life. What do you think?

First attempt

Underwater platform

Start

Water has been whitened so rat cannot see platform

Eighth attempt

Underwater platform

Start

At first, rats take a while to find the platform. But over several tries, they learn where it is.

The Morris water maze experiment is often used to test rats' abilities. It is perfectly suited to brown rats because they are good swimmers.

Working with Rats

Rats' amazing abilities mean they can sometimes do things humans cannot do. Like dogs, rats can combine their amazing sense of smell with their learning abilities and learn to detect particular scents. Some rats help doctors by spotting the smell of diseases such as **tuberculosis**. In war zones in Africa, giant pouched rats have been trained to sniff out **land mines**, so that they can be safely removed.

A rat learns to detect the smell of tuberculosis by sniffing samples of spit taken from patients.

A tight squeeze

One rat (named Rattie) in California has even been trained to help wire up school computer networks, by pulling a string along inside walls and ceilings to guide the cables into place. Rats' ability to get through narrow gaps could be used for other things, too, such as helping to find people trapped in mines, caves, or collapsed buildings.

This giant pouched rat is trained to sniff for land mines in Africa.

RAT STARS

Rats also work in entertainment. You might have seen them doing tricks in circus or street shows, and directors can book specially trained rats to perform in movies or on television.

Copying Rats

You might think of a robot as human-shaped, but more and more scientists are building robots inspired by animals. They include "ratbots," or rat robots.

Ratbots

Most ratbots focus on a special rat feature that humans do not have—super-sensitive whiskers. Robots with thin, flexible, plastic whiskers can sense their surroundings like a real rat. They could be used in hard-to-reach or dark places—to find earthquake survivors, for example.

In one experiment, real rat brain cells are being used to control robot rats. These ratbots are very simple at the moment, but they are revealing a lot about how brain cells learn and grow.

This scientist is showing the ratbot Psikharpax, named after a cunning rat in an old legend.

Remote-controlled rats

Scientists have also created "remote-controlled" real live rats, by fitting electrical implants into their brains and sending wireless signals from a laptop to control them. It sounds like something from a science fiction movie, but the rats do not seem to be upset by the experience. This work could pave the way for remote-control devices for humans to do things such as help paralyzed people to control their limbs.

Scientists were able to control the movements of this rat by giving it a sense of reward when it made a correct turn.

The Amazing Rat

Many people are afraid of or disgusted by rats. For centuries, rats have raided our food supplies, nibbled holes in our walls, and spread diseases. Sometimes, we have to take measures to control rat populations, or else they would take over our homes! So, rats and humans can be enemies.

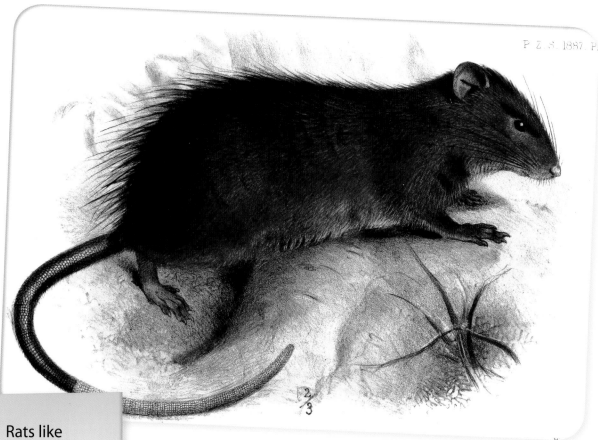

Rats like this one became **extinct** in 1903.

But maybe after reading this book, you will see rats in a different light! We have only recently realized how intelligent rats are. By working together with rats, at least some of the time, we can learn more about their amazing abilities.

Rat superpowers

If you could pick one of the rat's amazing superhuman abilities, which would you choose?

- If you had super-sensing whiskers like a rat's, you could easily feel your way in the dark and you'd constantly be sensing the textures all around you. You would look strange, though!

- If you had ultrasonic hearing like a rat's, you could listen to sounds made by bats, rats, dolphins, and other ultrasonic animals, but you would probably be annoyed by sounds from computers and gadgets that people cannot normally hear.

- If you had scent signal detection like a rat's, you could find anything you had lost by sniffing it out, and you could track down a snack easily.

- If you had an amazing rat tail, you could balance as you ran along rooftops—which is useful for escaping crowds on the sidewalk!

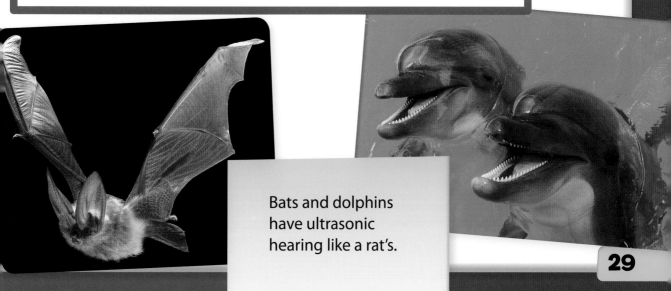

Bats and dolphins have ultrasonic hearing like a rat's.

Glossary

captive   held in a zoo, aquarium, or laboratory instead of living in the wild

dominant   having the most power and control

endangered   at risk of dying out

extinct   has died out forever

groom   clean the fur or skin

land mine   small bomb designed to go off when someone steps on it

mammal   type of warm-blooded animal that has a backbone, feeds on its mother's milk when young, and has hair on its body

nocturnal   active at night

obesity   state of being very overweight

pack   group of rats that live together

pheromone   chemical released from an animal's body to send a message

rodent   type of small, furry mammal. Rats, mice, squirrels, and hamsters are all rodents.

species   particular type of living thing

strains   types of animal within the same species, but with different features

tuberculosis   disease that can destroy the lungs or other body parts

ultrasonic   too high pitched for humans to hear naturally

Find Out More

Books

Day, Trevor. *The Secret Life of Rats: Rise of the Rodents* (Fact Finders: Extreme!). Mankato, Minn.: Capstone, 2008.

Savage, Stephen. *Rat* (Animal Neighbors). New York: PowerKids, 2009.

Whitehouse, Patricia. *Rats* (What's Awake?). Chicago: Heinemann Library, 2010.

Web sites

www.afrma.org
For expert advice, tips, and things to think about if you are considering a pet rat, take a look at the American Fancy Rat & Mouse Association's web site.

www.apopo.org/cms.php?cmsid=107
Learn all about the organization that trains giant pouched rats to sniff out land mines.

www.pestworldforkids.org/rats.html
Learn lots of facts about rats on this Pestworld for Kids web site.

Places to visit

You can see black, brown, and other rats at many zoos, including:

Philadelphia Zoo
3400 West Girard Avenue
Philadelphia, Pennsylvania 19104-1196
www.philadelphiazoo.org

Smithsonian National Zoo
3001 Connecticut Avenue NW
Washington, D.C. 20008
nationalzoo.si.edu

Index